SUCCESS THROUGH APPRECIATION

Jonathan P White

DEDICATION

This book is dedicated to my wife Joell, who practices appreciation and gratitude every day and showed me how much power it has...

BOOKS BY JONATHAN WHITE

Everyone Said I Should Write A Book

The Travels And Adventures Of A Sailor And Explorer

Everyone Said I Should Write Another Book

More Travels And Adventures Of A Sailor And Explorer

Everyone Said I Should Write A Third Book

Blimey! Even More Travels And Adventures Of A Sailor And Explorer
(Available Summer 2014)

Success Through Appreciation

Proven Methods To Grow Any Business Through Recognition And
Appreciation

All books are published by JoJo Publishing and are available on
Amazon.com and Kindle.

('Everyone Said I Should Write A Book' is also available on
Audible.com and iTunes, narrated by the author).

CONTENTS

ACKNOWLEDGEMENTS

To Kody who invented the system I use every day to reach out and appreciate people. Jordan who soars with it, Jules who embraced it and shares her enthusiasm with everyone, Dave and Shelly who introduced us to it ...

PREFACE

This short book was written with only one purpose - to increase your business. It is not a definitive answer to all your marketing needs but addresses three particular areas.

How do you retain your new clients? How do you maintain a loyal client base? How do you generate quality referrals?

I use the word client throughout, but it refers to anyone who provides the source of your income – customers, patients, clients, patrons, purchasers etc.

The simple, almost anachronistic method I suggest can be used by sales professionals, small and large business owners, doctors, attorneys, massage therapists, mechanics, hairdressers, service businesses, bankers…most likely, you, or you wouldn't be reading this book.

Any business or profession which relies on others to provide an income stream (and that's just about every one!) can and should be utilizing the age-old principles I suggest.

Besides employing it in your business life, the simple techniques I suggest can also make your personal life richer and more meaningful …

h

CHAPTER I

WHAT IS SUCCESS?

It sounds like a redundant question but most people have no precise idea what success means for them. Perhaps it's some vague amount of money, or a new home, or college for their kids or a comfortable retirement. But unless you specifically define what success means for you, how can you possibly achieve it?

If you asked fifty people to tell you right now what success signifies for them, how many could without having to think about it for five minutes? Can you? Most people can't and flounder through their years leading lives of quiet desperation, a couple of paychecks away from homelessness. Ninety five percent of baby boomers don't have enough money to retire with dignity.

Recently I met a dynamic young sales woman at a Chamber of Commerce meeting. She was excited to know the principles described in this book. Over a cup of coffee the first thing I asked in casual conversation was what her goals were? She looked at me with a blank expression.

"What do you mean?" she asked.

"Well, what do you want to achieve, where do you see yourself in a year, in five years?"

"Er, I don't know. Never thought about it, really. I don't have any goals."

No matter how dynamic she is, how attractive, how 'focused' on her sales job, by not having defined her goals, her dreams, her aspirations I believe she has doomed herself to mediocrity. How can she get where she wants to be when she doesn't even know where that is?

No matter your age, you need to have a goal, a dream, a 'why'. There are dozens of books and CD's by well-known inspirational speakers such as Tony Robbins who provide more detailed ideas and practices on setting and achieving goals – that's not what I'm going to do here. But I will suggest the basics...

Buy a journal. Doesn't have to be fancy, a spiral notebook will do. Write down three goals – what you want to accomplish in the next four weeks, in the next twelve months and in the next ten years. Use a separate page for each goal. Be specific. Envision what it will feel like. Write that down.

Be realistic – don't write 'I want to be a million dollars richer next month'. Chances are that won't happen and you'll just be discouraged. Even if it's something relatively easy, like 'I want to lose two pounds in four weeks', write it down. Then write what it will take to accomplish that. 'I'll walk a mile twice a day'. 'I'll stop eating doughnuts'. Whatever you know you can do to start off with.

At the end of the four weeks, write down how close you are to reaching that objective–be honest. If you aren't true to yourself with a small goal, how can you expect to reach the major ones? If you accomplish that goal, write that down. Pat yourself on the back, feel good. But don't eat a doughnut! Then write another goal...

Each month, on the first of the month write a specific, realistic goal for that month. 'Spend an extra hour a week with the kids', 'take my spouse out for a surprise dinner', 'acquire one new client a week'. Whatever it is, write it down and *just do it*! This will get you into the mindset of accomplishing what you set out to do.

If you want to be worth a million dollars in three years, expand on it. What's your plan to achieve that goal? Will you need to create other income streams, develop your business, get further education? What will you do with the million dollars? How does it make you feel? What are you willing to give up to achieve it - that new car you want right now, the trip to Tahiti next summer, time?

You can change your goals or add to them. Set a daily goal, a weekly goal, whatever works for you. But always write them down. There is a power that comes with the written word.

Write down the date that you intend reaching that goal. <u>Without a specific date, a goal is just a wish...</u>

You *must* get in the mindset of seeing your goals being achieved. You have to 'know' that whatever it is you're aiming for, you're on the way to getting there. No doubts, no excuses, no fear...

Stop using the word 'hope' – it's indecisive, like 'maybe'. Substitute the word 'intend' for hope. Get the word 'try' out of your vocabulary. Not 'I'll try to do that'. Instead 'I'll DO that'. It leaves you and everyone else with no doubt that you will do what you say. <u>'Hoping' and' trying' give you an excuse for not accomplishing.</u>

Make yourself a vision board. Cut out pictures of your goals – that car, that house, that vacation spot, the Ivy League college all your kids will attend, that million dollars... get a cork board and pin them to it. Hang it in a place you'll see it every day.

Get it in your mind that these things are already yours. If you don't feel that way, how can you expect them to happen?

Don't let anyone sway you from your dreams. If you don't feel others will understand and be totally supportive, don't tell them your dreams. Most people will feel threatened by someone who has a purpose and real goal in life – because they don't. They don't want to get out of their comfort zones and having a goal, a dream, a vision usually involves doing something new, different, perhaps a little unpleasant. And that's often scary...

Just be you...there's only one you in the whole world. Wake up each morning and look at your vision board. It's your "why', your reason to go to work, to strive, to be...

"You've got to have a dream, if you don't have a dream, how you gonna have a dream come true?"*

*'Happy Talk'. Rodgers & Hammerstein. 'South Pacific'. 1958

4

CHAPTER 2

WHY YOU NEED NEW CLIENTS

Every business person needs to attract new clients. It doesn't matter if you're a car dealer, a doctor or dentist, an insurance agency, a veterinarian, a banker, a lawyer, a contractor, a financial advisor – it makes no difference. It's all about sales.

What are those TV commercials really doing when professionals such as lawyers and dentists tout their services? Telling you they're such nice guys to do business with? They're selling to you. Yes, they have studied for years to get qualified, but they still need clients, they still need to attract new ones – they're sales people, too.

If you're a sales professional, you're always handing out business cards, networking, trying to meet new people, knocking on doors...

You need new clients to replace those who no longer use your services. Whether it's because they move out of the area (Americans move an average of once every six years!), they die, your competition lures them away... Whatever the cause (and you'll be surprised at the number one reason), you will have attrition.

You also want your business to grow. To do that there must be a continual stream of new clients. Some of them will decide after one encounter that they won't use your service again. Some will feel they had such a positive experience that they wouldn't go anywhere else. And most will fall somewhere in between.

The basic reason is that without clients you will have no business and make no money. Period.

So, how do you attract them? Today, most businesses have an internet presence. It's usually the first place you go to find the service you're looking for. And then you'll probably look at the reviews. That's why sites like 'Angie's List' are so successful. People want reassurance from others that they're making the right decision, whether it's for a realtor, plumber, insurance agent etc. Google is the new yellow pages.

But one of the problems with the Google world is that those looking for your business will also instantly see your competition. And if they're placed higher on the page or have more positive reviews, you can be overlooked in an instant.

You can advertise for new clients. Companies spend thousands, hundreds of thousands, millions of dollars to keep their name in front of you. You are bombarded by so much advertising through so many mediums these days, that it becomes a blur. Very few messages get through and stick in your mind. And it's a fact that, especially with print your ad has to be seen at least six times before it registers in your mind!

You can network and interact with others in your community. Join your local Chamber of Commerce, usually a good way to meet different business people. Go to meetup.com and find activities that interest you, where you can make new friends who may need your service. Expand your sphere of influence...

If you can't personally attend, ask an employee to represent you (don't forget to *appreciate* them each time with at least a thank you note and a small gift – *appreciating and recognizing* your employees is one key to growing your business). But as with anything, you get out of it what you put in. If you join an organization and don't participate, don't show your face on a regular basis, how can you expect it to work for you?

The most effective way to attract new clients is through the recommendation of current clients. The most valuable asset your business has is the satisfied clients you have worked so hard to attract and keep. They are your best sales force and if they feel they are *appreciated* they will refer you to their friends, family and business associates.

If you have ten clients on January 1 and each of those people feels *appreciated* by you and refer you one new client that month, then on January 31, you will have twenty clients. If those twenty all refer one new client in February, then on February 28 your business has grown to forty clients. Extrapolate that out until December 31 and see how your business (and your income) has grown. Of course, this isn't a perfect world and it's highly unlikely it will happen that way, but what if only ten percent of your clients referred you one new client a month?

Do you know how much it costs for you to attract a new client who is not a referral? I recently watched an episode of a popular TV show called 'Shark Tank'. Mark Cuban, a self-made billionaire businessman, asked a woman who wanted one of the 'sharks' to invest in her fledgling business, what was the cost of acquiring a customer? She didn't know... and she didn't get the investment.

What are some of those acquisition costs? Advertising, promotion, discounts, sales staff, gas mileage, dues to marketing organizations, postage, web site...

Studies have concluded that it costs between five and ten times more to obtain a new client than it does to retain an old one. That is a huge expense! What if you could eliminate that expense or at least reduce it substantially? Your bottom line would go up, right?

Many businesses rely on salespeople to acquire new clients. How successful are they? Do you or your sales manager, if you have one, really know how effective your sales people are, how many times a prospect is contacted, how much follow up they do? A study by the U.S. Small Business Administration in conjunction with the U.S. Chamber of Commerce discovered that:

- 2% of sales are made on the first call
- 3% are made on the second call
- 5% on the third call
- 10% on the fourth call
- 80% of all sales are made on the 5th – 12th call!

Those sales are a direct result of the number of contacts that are made. Be honest – how much follow up do you do with each prospect? Are you afraid of rejection? If you are, you need to investigate the power of 'no' and go for it. The more 'no's you get each day, the more 'yes's you'll get (that's a whole other topic!)...

The same study showed that:

- 48% of salespeople never follow up
- 25% make a second contact
- 12% make a third contact
- 10% make more than three contacts

Study those numbers. They don't need any explanation, they speak for themselves. If you're a professional sales person, where do you fit? Can you do better, especially if it's to achieve your 'why'?

There is a huge amount of potential business left on the table every day! Your business, your income, your future...

CHAPTER 3

HOW TO RETAIN CLIENTS

So you acquired a new client. Whether it's through your efforts or those of your sales staff, a walk-in, a purchased lead or a referral, another income stream has appeared. This person represents 'x' amount of dollars to you initially and over their lifetime. But if you keep this new client and they're happy with the service you provide, they could be worth five or ten or twenty times 'x'.

It's because satisfied clients love to tell others when they've found a great mechanic or hairdresser or insurance agent or doctor. Everyone does it – think how many times you couldn't wait to tell a friend about the new restaurant that has terrific food and reasonable prices, the chiropractor who eased your pain, the computer store that got rid of that virus.

When you consider how important each new client is to your success and growth, that they know dozens of people who may need your service, then isn't it vital to ensure that they are happy with your service; that they feel *appreciated*?

It's not the purpose of this book to tell you how to run your business. I'll assume you have a good product or service, that you respond to customer complaints promptly and effectively, that people need what you provide. I won't tell you how to advertise to attract new business or how to train your staff. But I will suggest one simple, effective way that will keep your clients loyal and have them raving to everyone they know, that you're the company to do business with.

What makes me want to use your company, your product, your service again and again, even if I can find it cheaper somewhere else? Why do *you* go to the same dry cleaner, use the same insurance agent, drive a little out of your way to find that piece of hardware?

The main reason why (and we may not even be conscious of it) is that we feel *appreciated*. We feel *recognized* and valuable. In this disconnected world, it feels great to know that the clerk remembers your name, that they smile at you, that you're acknowledged and made to feel important.

But it has to be genuine and it has to be personal. When my wife worked at a large marine retail store many years ago, she was instructed to always say "Welcome to …. Marine" to everyone who walked past her, coming into the store. It didn't matter if she was involved with another client. Not genuine, not personal…

It happens every day in most 'big box' stores. Some even have a dedicated greeter to make you feel appreciated. Does it work? Probably not. It's usually cursory, meaningless, merely rote and we all know the only reason they're doing this is because corporate sent out a memo! That isn't *appreciation*, it's unlikely to keep you coming back and sometimes it's even intrusive and annoying!

But if you are made to feel truly *appreciated*, if you are greeted by name, if you get a surprise birthday card in your mail box , if you are viewed as a valuable asset and treated that way, then the chances are much higher that you will remain a loyal client and tell others.

It's not a new concept, it's even written about in all the great religious books, including the bible. It's so simple, it's almost taken for granted but with most businesses, it's not even practiced. It seems a little outdated, somewhat anachronistic. It's called gratitude. It means being thankful for having you as a client. It means *appreciating* that I am important to you and your business.

Why would I use your service again if I felt that I was just a number? Would I tell my friends or business associates that they should choose you, when there are so many choices today? You have to be memorable, you have to be 'top of mind'. What does that mean? As soon as I think, "I need an oil change", your business should be the only one I would consider, even if Joe's Garage down the street has a 'special' for half off.

If it's time to hire a payroll company and you're one of several who've solicited me, I'm probably going to choose the one who made me feel important, who stays in touch, who lets me know that I will be *appreciated* if I become their client.

If my brother wants insurance, I will refer him to your agency right away, because I know you will *appreciate* him as much as you've *appreciated* me. If my friend hurt their back and needs a chiropractor, I'm going to immediately suggest they call you, because you're 'top of mind' for that need.

This is why each client is worth far more to you in the long term than just their immediate business.

So how do you *appreciate* your clients and prospects **effectively, consistently and on a personal level?** What are some of the options?

It's the computer age, right? You'll send an email, maybe use a 'drip campaign' to stay in touch. An impersonal email goes out every two or four weeks, inviting them to use your service. (Some companies send them daily!). And you'll offer a discount, let your client know there's a 'special'; they'll be really happy to know that and will rush over and do business immediately! Right...

That doesn't work on a number of levels. First, offering a deal, a discount, a 'special' is not showing *appreciation* or gratitude. It's about them, not you. It's almost begging – "Please come in, I need business so desperately, I'll offer you 15% off". That's usually a turn-off.

Second – it's an email! Years ago, when the internet first started, emails were a novelty (I'm sure most of you don't remember a world without email or the internet!). How many emails do you receive every day? And what happens to most of them, especially unsolicited ones? 'Delete'.

So your ineffective message doesn't even get read most of the time. The perception of unsolicited business emails that make it past the spam filter is that they're intrusive and unnecessary. I delete them without reading them and most likely, so do you.

What about using the mail? Everyone goes to their mailbox. You'll get your message of *appreciation* out that way. You'll send all your clients a letter saying how much they mean to you. (And you'll also let them know you're offering a special because they're such loyal clients!).

So you have a letter made up on your letterhead. And it goes into a business sized envelope which of course has your company logo and address in the top left corner. And because you have a great contact manager and state-of-the-art printer, it's easy to stick on a thousand computer generated address labels to the front of the envelopes. Then you use your franking machine to put the postage on. It looks very impressive – to you.

But what does it look like when your client gets their mail? What does it look like to you when you sort through your mail standing over the waste bin? That's right; it looks like a business letter. You *may* open it, you may quickly glance at it, but it's printed in Times New Roman or some other easily recognizable business font and you'll probably toss it.

The same with postcards; in fact it's more likely that a postcard will get thrown out after being briefly scanned. You know right away it's from a business or service. They're probably offering some deal, maybe you'll stick it in a drawer – where it will be discovered a year later!

I know, I'll call them on the phone, just to say hello and let them know I appreciate their business! Great idea! Let's assume that you get through the 'gate keeper', who is either a real person or an answering device. What will you say?

"Mr. Jones, this is Tom Jenkins!"

"Who?"

"Tom. From the framing shop. You came in last month to have a picture framed..."

"OK? Ah, is there a problem with my credit card or something?"

"No, no, Mr. Jones. Just a quick call to let you know how much I appreciate your business!"

"Er, right, Bob, I mean Tom. Look I'm busy right now, thanks for the call. 'Bye."

If you got a phone call like that, would you look at your phone with a puzzled look after you hung up? Not only was that call obtrusive and ineffective, your customer now thinks you're a bit of a nut case...

But let's take this scenario one step further, into the realm of the ridiculous!

So if emails, business letters, postcards and phone calls don't work...what does? How about face-to-face? You can tell your customer in person! You'll set aside a couple of hours after work each day and you and your staff will visit each of your clients and when they answer the door at their home, you'll greet them with a big smile and tell them how much you appreciate their business and how important they are to you, maybe hand them a business card...

That will keep you and your company top of mind. Your client will also think you're out of your mind! If a mechanic from Spiffy Loob knocked on my door at 7:00 p.m. to tell me he appreciates my choosing his business to change my oil, I'd probably look incredulous, back off and close the door, hoping he wasn't totally insane. Then I'd watch him through the curtains to make sure he left...

So really, how important is it to stay top of mind, to let your clients know they're treasured? And if it is so vitally important to the growth of your business, how do you do it **effectively, consistently and on a personal level**?

"I've learned that people will forget what you said, people will forget what you did, but people will never forget how you made them feel." Maya Angelou

CHAPTER 4

WHY DO YOU LOSE CLIENTS?

There are a few ways this happens. Some of them you have control over, some of them you don't. Remember the survey in Chapter 2? The one conducted by the government agency and the U.S. Chamber of Commerce? During their questioning they discovered some interesting facts about why businesses lose clients:

- 1%   die
- 3%   move
- 5%   go with a friends' recommendation
- 9%   price
- 14% product dissatisfaction

Two of those reasons, the first two, are beyond your control. If you have a client who is loyal, really loyal, who feels *appreciated*, then perhaps your percentage of number three will be slightly less. But just as some people will use your service because they were recommended by a friend, so will an equal number use a competitor recommended by that friend.

You may be able to save some clients by lowering your price, but then you lower your profit. Can you afford to do that on a consistent basis? Most clients are willing to pay a little more if they feel they are valued and important.

Which leads to the (so far) largest percentage of lost clientele. Product dissatisfaction encompasses not just a shabby item or poor service, but also how an unhappy client is handled. If the item purchased is defective, then replacing it with the minimum inconvenience and hassle can usually rectify that and you won't necessarily have lost a customer. Especially if as soon as this happens, the client is made to feel *appreciated*.

If you lose a client because of poor customer service, that's ultimately your problem. Unless you resolve the situation immediately, the chances are you'll never gain that client back. The initial effects may be small – one lost client.

But with the advent of Yelp and so many online reviews, there's no telling how far the damage can spread and what impact it will have on your future earnings. Assuming you can address the issue immediately and save the client, then you must go out of your way to show them *appreciation*. You must do something that will re-establish you as the only business to use in your field. You have to make an impactful statement. Later in this book, I'll make suggestions on how to do this...

Going back to the statistics above, if you total up the percentage of reasons why you lose clients you'll see that it comes to 32%.

What about the rest? What's the number one reason that the vast majority of your clients, even those who've been loyal for a long time, will leave you and seek out your competitor, according to the U.S. Small Business Administration and the U.S. Chamber of Commerce? The reason is:

'Perceived indifference'.

Two words that can make or break your business. No matter how much you like or even love your clients, no matter how important you know each one is, if *they* don't know that, if that's not conveyed **effectively and consistently on a personal level**, the perception is that they don't matter to you.

And whether or not <u>you</u> believe you're showing them *appreciation*, if your clients/customers/patients don't 'get' that, if it's not communicated to them **effectively and consistently on a personal level**, then the perception is that you don't care if they do business with you or not.

And if you don't *appreciate* them, your competitors will...

CHAPTER 5

WHAT WORKS?

By now you should understand why you need to *recognize* and *appreciate* your clients **effectively, consistently and on a personal level**. When you do, there are two direct results.

First it's much more likely that your current clients will stay with you. Wouldn't you continue to use the services of a business that *appreciates* you and makes you feel important?

Second and much more important to the growth of your business, is that a happy client will likely want to share his positive experience with his friends, family and business associates. Studies have concluded that most adults know about a thousand people by their first name. I think that's a lot, probably some know that many and some don't. So, let's cut that down drastically to 200 people, twenty percent.

Suppose our happy client shares his experience with only ten percent of those people. He tells twenty friends he knows, over a period of time, that he found a great mechanic, a terrific dentist, a caring vet. And perhaps ten percent of those people will take his advice when they're looking for those services. Now that one client has provided you two more at no cost to you. If you refer back to the figures on page 7 about how quality referrals can grow your business, and extrapolate it out you'll discover that in a year or two your client base has grown and grown...

What if those numbers doubled, what if each happy, *appreciated* client referred four people to you and they eventually each refer four people? And you treat them well providing stand-out service and first-rate products. And you *recognize* and *appreciate* them **effectively, consistently and on a personal level.** Now you will have a spreading network of people growing your business or practice for you – in other words a large, unpaid sales force!

Don't take my word for it. Go to your computer and Google 'Joe Girard'. If you know who he is, you know where I'm going with this. If you don't, he is the greatest car salesman who ever lived.

He averaged selling six new Chevrolets every day for fifteen years - at retail! He's in the Guinness Book of World Records. People drove hundreds of miles just to buy a car from him! How did he do it?

It's very simple. He built relationships with people. He let them know **effectively, consistently and on a personal level** that each and every person was important to him and he *appreciated* their trust in him. He did it by a simple, inexpensive, effective method.

He sent thank you notes and greeting cards! Every month and an extra one for Christmas. He knew how important it was to keep 'top of mind' when his customers needed a new car. And back in the late sixties and seventies, most people bought a new car every two years.

And what did those *appreciated*, *recognized*, valued clients do? They told their friends about this great salesman who said 'hello' every month in their mailbox and remembered them at Christmas. And some people, even if they weren't planning on buying a Chevy, would buy one just so they could feel *appreciated* by Joe Girard...

And if the internet had been available back then, Joe probably wouldn't have used it – emails miss one of the key ingredients necessary to grow a referral-based business. They're not personal.

Here's a rhetorical question. It's your birthday. You receive four real cards in the mail and twenty ecards on your computer screen. Who do you think *really* cares about you? When they first came out, everyone thought ecards were the greatest thing. But that was a long time ago and now they're just viewed as a free, ineffective, impersonal way to show someone you 'care'. And they usually get deleted quickly.

Joe Girard is just one example of thousands of prosperous business people who understand that relationships are vital to their success. And that nothing cements a relationship better than showing *appreciation* **effectively, consistently and on a personal level...**

Big business understands how important customer loyalty is – look at the proliferation of 'loyalty programs' out there today. You get free air miles if you stick with the airline or one of its partners. Discounts on Smell gasoline if you use their credit card. Buy nine Tubway sandwiches and get the tenth for free. There are dozens of variants with the same idea - keep 'em coming back!

Are they effective? Probably, to some extent. Otherwise they'd disappear, just like 'Green Stamps' did (if you know what I'm referring to, you're showing your age!). But who pays for them? You, the consumer. They cost a fortune to administer and the cost of the 'giveaways' has to be borne by someone – and it's not the shareholders!

If they would *recognize* how important their current clients are and *appreciate* them on a personal level, rather than constantly trying to attract new clients, then I believe their business would grow and sustain that growth.

If you're 'big business', then you may not care if you have unhappy, unappreciated, dissatisfied clients. You can afford to lose them and will just get more.

How? Advertising, of course. Bombard the airwaves with mindless, marginally true commercials. Pollute the beauty of the country with billboards, clog the internet with pop-ups and spam, fill the mailbox with junk...

Someone once said, "In America, everyone is either buying or selling...all the time."

CHAPTER 6

WHY IT WORKS

A basic human need is to feel of value, to feel special, to feel *appreciated*. We all respond to a kind word, a hug, a word of encouragement. Whether it's on a personal level from family or friends, it always feels good to be acknowledged for doing something nice or showing kindness or gratitude, or just for being who we are.

In the workplace there's nothing like simple *recognition* to put a smile on the face of an employee. And when you do, especially if you do it **effectively, consistently and on a personal level** the benefits to you and your business are long lasting and incalculable.

You've heard the expression – 'the world is shrinking'. Well, in terms of connections, it certainly is. We're more in touch, we have more electronic devices, Facebook, internet, twitter, texting… everything to link us to each other faster and more efficiently.

People spend inordinate amounts of time communicating on their devices. And there's no doubt that the information age is helping those who are connected to it. The effects of social media are exploding across the planet. Now we can find old friends, meet new ones, share experiences, help each other…

But there's a downside as well. This rapid, pervasive connectivity also leads to a big disconnect. It's all 'two dimensional', it's not real human contact, it's cyber connectivity. And a lot if it is written in a language that further disconnects. Abbreviations, word shortening, practically hieroglyphics! It's hard to feel *appreciated* on a computer screen or via a text message.

For a lot of people, there is a certain dread about checking their email first thing in the morning. How many messages will there be today, all demanding your attention? Sometimes it's like triage in an emergency room! How will you get through it all? And no one *appreciates* that you're doing all this...

Not only does perceived indifference negatively affect your clients, it can also have a detrimental effect on your employees. Remember, everyone needs to feel *appreciated*, even if it's just simple *recognition*. An email won't do it!

Why was Joe Girard so successful that he had to hire people to help him show *appreciation* and keep his 'gratitude' system running smoothly? Because he *recognized* how vital it is to *recognize*. And he valued the people who worked for him, he *appreciated* them. And guess what, they worked harder for him...

The fact is, he made everyone feel important. And when you make someone feel important they stand taller, feel prouder, work harder, are happier. And he did it with greeting cards and thank you notes!

Up until a few years ago I had sent maybe twenty-five cards my whole life. And that was only because my mum insisted! But once I realized the power of a thank you note, once I understood the concept of *appreciating* my client base, once I saw my business start to grow through quality referrals from *appreciated* clients, I sent cards every day! I became a card-sending maniac and it paid off in my business world and in my personal life as well. I still send cards and probably always will...

Every day I send at least one heartfelt greeting card, a real one, not an ecard, and some days I send a dozen or more. Do I get writer's cramp? Not in this computer generated age! There are a few companies out there who have clever systems that allow you to create a real card on your computer and with the click of a key, they print, stuff, address, attach a stamp and take it to the post office!

This not only cuts down dramatically on the time necessary to choose and write cards, but with the (free!) system I use, it's much cheaper and a lot more convenient than going to the store. I can even use my own handwriting and signature!

And there's no doubt this is a positive thing to do on a number of levels. From the sender's point of view, it's wonderful to know that you're doing something to make someone feel *appreciated*. Personally, it sets me up for the day knowing that in a few days, someone will get a surprise when they go through their mail.

I enjoy the creative process and the system I use allows me to be artistic if I want. Or I can choose from a catalogue of thousands of stock cards. It also allows me to send a small gift or gift card – this really makes an impression on a wavering prospect or special client! Talk about a client for life and quality referrals!

On the recipient's end, when they go through their mail (most of which is junk!) they'll find a personalized envelope, greeting card size. "Wait, it's not my birthday", is usually the initial thought. But I guarantee it will get opened. And that's where a greeting card triumphs over a business letter or postcard. It gains their attention and they want to look at it. First barrier overcome – it will not get tossed out.

When they remove a high-quality 'Thank You' or 'Nice To Meet You' card (and it must be high quality, a discount card won't do!) with a few simple words of *appreciation*, it will generate a smile. Even if it's just for a second, you've positively impacted that person's life, made them feel important, *appreciated*. And the likelihood is, they will keep the card, put it on their desk, even if it's just for a day.

If the system you choose allows you to, like mine does, always upload a nice photo of yourself in the card. Talk about 'top of mind'…

So your prospect or client has the card, a three-dimensional object, not some pixels on a computer screen, in their hand and they're looking at it. What should you say? What should they read? What's the message you want to get across?

What's the key word in this book? **_Appreciation._**

Just say 'Thank you':

- Thank you for taking the time to meet with me about how my company can be of service to you.

- Thank you for putting your trust in me to handle your finances.

- I appreciate you bringing your car to my shop for service. I look forward to a long and positive relationship.

- Thank you for the referral. It means a lot to me that you have recommended your friend. Here's a Starbucks gift card, have a coffee on me. (That really works!).

- I really appreciate all you do to keep my business/practice running smoothly. Please share these delicious brownies with the staff. (_Recognize_ your employees, regularly!)

These are just some suggestions of what you could say. The possibilities are endless. But it's equally important what you shouldn't say. Remember, this is strictly about a_ppreciation…_

Don't say:

- Thanks for using my business. I'm offering a 10% discount to my best clients and you're one of them!

- Bring in this card for a special gift!

- Send me a referral and you get a free oil change!

- Hey, it was great meeting you at the network event. Check out my website...

It's NOT about promoting your business (although if you *appreciate* rather than promote, that's exactly the end result!). When you *appreciate* someone and make them feel good, they will automatically want to do business with you and if you reach out to them **effectively, consistently and on a personal level**, you will have a client for life.

Don't take my word for it. Put yourself in the position of the recipient. How would it make you feel if you received a simple *appreciation* card in the mail? Especially if you were having a bad day. It would change your mind set, even if it's only for a minute or two. Might put a smile on your face. Would definitely make you feel valued. Would definitely reinforce that you wouldn't think of getting your oil changed somewhere else, that's the only dentist you'll ever use, you're glad you chose this financial advisor... That's being **personal**.

Now imagine what it would do for your business if you reached out to your clients every two or three months! Again, no advertising, no promotional offers, no 'special deals'. Even if you haven't seen them in a while. Especially if you haven't seen them in a while!

This is where the word **consistently** applies. Just as in advertising, you have to continually market yourself in order to remain competitive, to be 'top of mind', so you must **consistently** reach out to your client base.

Some of the computer generated systems have a 'drip campaign' feature which allows you to send out a different card on a pre-programmed date to your clients. I usually got a phone call when a client received the first card, thanking me for being so thoughtful. And when I sent them a small gift or gift card, I always received at least an email, sometimes another phone call! That's being **effective**…

'Appreciation Wins Over Promotion…*Every Time!*'

CHAPTER 7

WHAT WILL IT DO?

Very simply, it will grow your business. It won't happen overnight, it's not a 'get-rich-quick' scheme, not a way to necessarily increase the bottom line immediately–although that has certainly happened! But you will notice the difference, as your clients comment on your thoughtfulness and *appreciation*.

You will see an increase in quality referrals as they tell their friends and associates. And if you treat these new clients/customers/ patients the same, if you reach out to them with *appreciation* ***effectively, consistently and on a personal level***, they will send you more business. It's like a healthy tree with more branches and leaves spreading out and growing. And it's growing your business!

How much more business can you expect? That's a very subjective question. What do you do? Attorney, doctor, massage therapist, mechanic, financial advisor, sales rep, mechanic? How long have you been doing it? Are you just starting out? How many clients do you have? Do you have their mailing addresses (not just their email address)? Do you have a contact manager? How much are you willing to invest in a client in order to *appreciate* him/her and generate quality referrals?

If you don't have their mailing address, a simple way to obtain it is to ask when is their birthday? Not their birth date – you don't need to find out how old they are! Just the month and day. Tell them you LOVE to send <u>real</u> birthday cards. Everyone enjoys getting a card on their birthday! If they say no, let it go. Doesn't matter, most people will gladly give it to you. Then ask for their mailing address...Simple!

Think how they'll react when they get an *appreciation* card from you and it's <u>not</u> their birthday...

Enter their address and birthday into your contact manager (the product I use has a free user-friendly system that reminds me of birthdays, anniversaries etc. It also enabled me to import my contacts from Excel.). And always send them a birthday card! If you can get their spouses' birthday, send them a card too!

Kids – absolutely! If you remember your clients' kids' birthdays every year, do you think he's going to go anywhere else? And what happens when the kids grow and need your service? Who do you think they'll use to fix their car, buy insurance from, hire as a realtor, an attorney, a dentist..?

What kind of an investment does it take to accomplish this? Half a dozen greeting cards a year per client. If you find the right product/system, it should cost you less than a dollar a card. Is it worth investing about ten dollars a year to *appreciate* each client? Only you can make that judgment...

From my experience (when I first started sending cards to my clients I owned a small advertising company), I saw a yearly increase of about 15% directly attributable to reaching out in *appreciation*. Talking to business owners who have used a similar system over a three-year period the consensus is that you can expect about a 12-20% increase in business. Maybe you'll have more, maybe less.

There's no scientific way to quantify your ROI, besides new clients specifically telling you that they're here because they were referred by a current client.

But there is no doubt that by practicing this simple idea ***effectively, consistently and on a personal level*** you will see results.

CHAPTER 8

APPRECIATION AND RECOGNITION IN YOUR PERSONAL LIFE

After sending greeting cards to my clients and getting positive feedback from them, my wife suggested I send a card to a friend who was sick.

Considering that I didn't have to drive to the store, stand in front of a rack of cards, find one that didn't really say what I wanted, wait in line to pay $3.99, drive home, write the words, address the envelope (after searching the address book), find a stamp (darn, we're out, have to go to the post office), mail the card...considering that I didn't have to do all that with the neat system I had used for my business, I created and sent the card in a minute from my computer for less than a dollar including postage!

When I got a phone call from Jeff a few days later telling me how thoughtful I was and how I had totally brightened his day, I realized that sending an unexpected, heartfelt card could be very impactful. I started gathering birthdays and anniversaries and sending cards to friends and family. I became a 'rock star' with everyone, the contact manager always reminding me to send that card.

But beyond that, I started to look for excuses to send cards! If I hear that someone has just lost a job, I'll send an upbeat, 'don't worry' card. If someone gets a promotion at work, I'll send a congratulations card. If the mother of an acquaintance is sick, I'll get their address and send a card. I send 'thank you' cards whenever someone does something nice.

I send cards to kids, not only for their birthdays – just to say how cool I think they are or congratulating them for an achievement at school. Their parents often call us and say their kids were thrilled to get a card addressed to them in the mailbox and it wasn't even their birthday!

Would I reach out, send all these cards if I had to go out to the store and go through the lengthy, annoying, expensive process described in the second paragraph of this chapter? Absolutely not!

But with the ability to send real greeting cards from my computer, at minimum cost and maximum convenience, I touch people all the time. What I started to do and continue to do today (and probably will forever), is send out something positive in an increasingly negative world.

Does it work? For my wife and I, it does. We both feel great when we create and send a card. We feel great because we know we're going to make a positive impact on someone in a few days. We feel great if we get acknowledged for doing it.

But reaching out in *appreciation* must be done with no expectation of any return. It must be done solely to show gratitude without being upset if no one responds.

In fact, your life will be a lot less stressful if you live without expectation. That doesn't mean you don't have goals, as mentioned in Chapter 1. It means you release the outcome; imagine it, write it down in your journal, set it in motion, intend it and just let it work out the way it will. All you can do in life is 'plant seeds'. You have no control over how they grow. Writing down your goals is one way of planting seeds.

So what happens when you express gratitude and *appreciation* and you do it with kindness and joy? I don't know what your beliefs are - that's not relevant. I do know that when you show gratitude it is returned to you, many times over; in your personal life and in your business world.

At the least, you've made someone feel good, feel *appreciated*, feel special. A tiny bit of positive energy in a world that desperately needs it. But there's no doubt, you'll strengthen personal relationships and grow your business. Think like Joe Girard – become financially successful by showing *appreciation*...

Effectively, Consistently and on a Personal Level

This book is available in paperback at www.amazon.com and on kindle devices.

Jonathan P White is an international entrepreneur who has started and grown businesses in six countries. He has also been a professional ocean sailor and is the author of two successful true-life adventure books. He currently lives on an island in Florida with his wife, Joell.

SUGGESTED READING

Go For No! Richard Fenton & Andrea Waltz. Courage Crafters, 2010.

The Charge. Brendon Burchard. Free Press, 2012.

The Magic. Rhonda Byrne. Atria Books, 2012.

Start With Why. Simon Sinek. Penguin, 2009.

Rain Making: Attract New Clients No Matter What Your Field. Ford Harding. Adams Media, 2008.

The 5 Languages of Appreciation in the Workplace: Empowering Organizations by Encouraging People. Gary Chapman. Northfield Publishing, 2012.

Focus on the Good Stuff: The Power of Appreciation. Mike Robbins. Jossey-Bass, 2010.

Everything by Tony Robbins!

www.ingramcontent.com/pod-product-compliance
Lightning Source LLC
Chambersburg PA
CBHW071548170526
45166CB00004B/1582

* 9 7 8 1 4 8 9 5 2 7 7 2 1 *